Blodeuwedd

To the Memory of John Tripp

Blodeuwedd

and other poems

TONY CONRAN

POETRY WALES PRESS
1988

POETRY WALES PRESS
GREEN HOLLOWS COTTAGE, CRAIG-YR-EOS ROAD,
OGMORE-BY-SEA, MID GLAMORGAN

British Library Cataloguing in Publication Data

Conran, Anthony, *1931–*
Blodeuwedd
I. Title
821'.914

ISBN 0-907476-78-3

Cover illustration:- 'Woodlands Interior' by Deran Fenwick

Cover Design by Jeane Rees

Published with the financial support of the
Welsh Arts Council

Typeset in 10½ point Plantin by Megaron, Cardiff
Printed by Antony Rowe Ltd., Chippenham

Contents

Acknowledgements

Some of these poems have appeared in *Poetry Wales*, *Anglo-Welsh Review*, *Wales in Verse*, *The Future of the Word* (the first WUW Register), *Fine Madness*, *Glas-nos*, *Cubi Si (The magazine of the Britain-Cuba Resource Centre)*, *On Censorship* (the second WUW Register), *Stand*, *Planet*, *Chanter* (the magazine of the Bagpipe Society), and *Random Order*. 'Elegy for the Welsh Dead' has been broadcast on Radio 3.

Blodeuwedd was produced and performed as a modern dance by Bronwyn Judge and Anna Holmes in Bangor and Swansea, featuring the paintings of Michael Cullimore which in large part inspired it. A second production, by the same dancers, toured New Zealand under the title, *Created Woman*.

I have included as an appendix the programme note for the New Zealand production, hoping it might prove useful. I apologise if some of it might seem obvious to readers living in Wales.

It is always possible that poems to or about named persons may give offence. That was not my intention. I was only concerned to do honour to those that I wrote for.

THIRTEEN WAYS OF LOOKING AT
A HOOVER

for Barbara Zanditon

i

The party suddenly condensed
To the four of us —
Him, and him and her, and me.

I have never seen anger so elegant!
He checkmates them
Lifting their legs
To hoover, ruthlessly, their chair-space.

ii

A hoover is like a camel —
It humps itself with provender
And can be trained to spit.

iii

One would hardly believe
That even four humans and two cats
Gave so much skin.

Yet, once a week,
The bloated paper intestine of this beast
Has to be emptied of our bits of death.

iv

The difficult slow ease of scything hay —
It is comparable
To her adroitness with its wheels and flex.

v

After many days of toothache
To be grateful for the amnesia
Of a dentist's chair.

And after the long chaos of builders,
Carpenters, electricians,
Destroyers of plaster —

To be sensuously grateful
For the din of a hoover.

vi

In their iron age
The antique hoovers
— All pistons and steel tubes and levers —
In our square-carpeted drawing-rooms
Did not disguise their alienation.

I once turned a corner in Liverpool
And saw, disappearing down a side-street,
A vast, black-leaded steam locomotive,
O-four-O, colossal amid cars.

The antique hoovers, one felt,
Were de-railed like that.

vii

Hoovers would like to be precise.
Their robot souls yearn for clearances
Plus or minus a thousandth of an inch.
Always, by wobble or pile or buffer,
They are betrayed. Your average yard-brush
Is more of a precision instrument!

viii

The soul of a hoover —
Is it the empty bag
That nothingness blows out like a sail?
Or is it the paradoxical geometry
Of the twisting belt, that burns
Sourly at the ingestion of a tack?

ix

There is a sub-culture of hoovers.
Hoovermen with wiry, terrier moustaches
Poke their heads from dusty limousines
To stop you in the road —

"That new belt I put in —
Has it remedied the fault?
Shall I come to see it?"

Their deft enquiries
Have strict authority over your thoughts.
They carry a king's seal, dispense his justice.

x

Its noise is more sensitive than you'd imagine.
It marks the difference between dusts.

xi

Most of us in a lifetime get to know
One, two, three hoovers. And that is enough.
We think we know the species.

But what of the professionals, the home-helps,
The Rent-a-maids from Hampstead?
Out of the hundreds of hoovers
Their fingers have caressed,
One, two, three stand out
Incomparable.

                    As they think of these
Majestic, suave, blond super-hoovers,
Their thighs grow supple with pride,
Their pupils take on the steady gleam
Of an enthusiast, they are fulfilled.

We don't know the half of what hoovers can do.

xii

On what authority you say it I don't know,
But you say, "The hoover has no Muse".
Yet from the murk and ashes of our common
Existence, the accumulating death
Of our lives together in this room,
The hoover creates darkness, order, love.
Its wake in the waves of a carpet
Makes lines of growth, furrows a field like a plough.

Could Erato of the laughing eyes, Urania,
Or Melpomene who bore to a slinky river-god
The enticing Sirens, half-girl, half-duck —

Could these *echt*-Muses have ordered it better?

xiii

It's a great virtue in hoovers
You can switch them off.

WILD FORM

for the wedding of Ellie and Steve

That's not a hydrangea, is it?
Yes, the wild form —
A floating raft of tiny pink
Peppercorns

And round it, like winds on a compass,
Huge sterile
Florets, velvet and crinoline
Like a waxwork smile.

It is the peppercorn buds mean business —
The real flowers,
Symmetrically accurate
Jabs of power.

Stamens prod out like the knobs
Of the Red Queen's crown.
They are the naked thing. Bees
Crowd down

To a consummation of damp pollen,
The bloom's
Orgasmic cry of colour
In a green room.

FERN AT YNYS LLANDDWYN

She crouches on an all-but island,
Rockface bedded in sheets of marram.

Grass stings like a hair shirt
Between muscles of the sand
And the wrenched steel of the wind.

She hides, sniffing the sea-spray.
It is a fern frontier, this coast
Where the grey schist erupts.

She watches the sky, a green girl
Pregnant with epiphytes
From the equatorial trees.

No, that's a daydream. She sniffs salt,
Keeps watch on the Wall.
She is fern on the frontiers of fern.

Though she tries bitterly to
Remember her exile from the jungle,
She could not live there.

Mothering sap swells into sandy groins.
She is native here. She answers
To the breathing of the tide.

ELEGY FOR THE WELSH DEAD, IN THE FALKLAND ISLANDS, 1982

Gŵyr a aeth Gatraeth oedd ffraeth eu llu.
Glasfedd eu hancwyn, a gwenwyn fu.
—*Y Gododdin* (6th century)

(Men went to Catraeth, keen was their company.
They were fed on fresh mead, and it proved poison.)

Men went to Catraeth. The luxury liner
For three weeks feasted them.
They remembered easy ovations,
Our boys, splendid in courage.
For three weeks the albatross roads,
Passwords of dolphin and petrel,
Practised their obedience
Where the killer whales gathered,
Where the monotonous seas yelped.
Though they went to church with their standards
Raw death has them garnished.

Men went to Catraeth. The Malvinas
Of their destiny greeted them strangely.
Instead of affection there was coldness,
Splintering iron and the icy sea,
Mud and the wind's malevolent satire.
They stood nonplussed in the bomb's indictment.

Malcolm Wigley of Connah's Quay. Did his helm
Ride high in the war-line?
Did he drink enough mead for that journey?
The desolated shores of Tegeingl,
Did they pig this steel that destroyed him?
The Dee runs silent beside empty foundries.
The way of the wind and the rain is adamant.

Clifford Elley of Pontypridd. Doubtless he feasted.
He went to Catraeth with a bold heart.
He was used to valleys. The shadow held him.
The staff and the fasces of tribunes betrayed him.
With the oil of our virtue we have annointed
His head, in the presence of foes.

Phillip Sweet of Cwmbach. Was he shy before girls?
He exposes himself now to the hags, the glance
Of the loose-fleshed whores, the deaths
That congregate like gulls on garbage.
His sword flashed in the wastes of nightmare.

Russell Carlisle of Rhuthun. Men of the North
Mourn Rheged's son in the castellated vale.
His nodding charger neighed for the battle.
Uplifted hooves pawed at the lightning.
Now he lies down. Under the air he is dead.

Men went to Catraeth. Of the forty-three
Certainly Tony Jones of Carmarthen was brave.
What did it matter, steel in the heart?
Shrapnel is faithful now. His shroud is frost.

With the dawn men went. Those forty-three,
Gentlemen all, from the streets and byways of Wales,
Dragons of Aberdare, Denbigh and Neath —
Figment of empire, whore's honour, held them.
Forty-three at Catraeth died for our dregs.

GIRL PREGNANT

Another being is at her gravity.
She is pulled to its purposes
Like a continent. Slowly, her flesh drifts.

Crops are re-distributed
As she passes through new climates.
Around her contours vineyards are turreted.

Sleepy volcanoes crouch in the haze of her.
She is well-watered. To the South
Deserts recede into mirage.

Slowly, under her heart, the rock piles up,
The mountains build, the kicking Alp
Hoists her into human air. Past — future —

Drift. She crowds into a destiny
That is not hers, though the bow of her
Slices the covering wave towards her child.

RESEARCH

In tasteful, inconspicuous buildings
Set about with shrubs and looking out
On ploughed fields, villages and woodlands,
Equitably they plot how to kill my children,
Marged and little Alys, six and three.

Those intelligent young men in the Ukraine
Would, if we met, show me photos
Of round-eyed daughters. They have nightmares —
Tasteful, inconspicuous buildings that
Cotoneasters and mock-orange decorate

Where people I pay arrive at nine most mornings
Busy to think out how to murder those
Ukrainian darlings all the livelong day,
From time to time resting their eyes
On fields and woods of Powys or Hertfordshire.

SNOWDROPS

The snow's gone, the green sinews
Of the world stretch in the woods.
Feeders of light come mewing.
Leaf puts its key to the lock.

From the bud's cornucopia,
From the coracle of the bulb,
The shy ones, the first merchants
Stand with their wares in the mould.

POTATOES

for Brace, a civil servant

Potato haulms grasp at the rain.
Gnarled hands
Like earthen dwarf hands, like gross
Seaweed fronds

Clutch at our low sky. Western promise
In the soil
Is waiting for glut. Rounding tubers
Await our toil.

Market forces dictate, not hunger.
To hold the price
We dye wide acres of them blue, leave them
For eelworm or mice.

At the other end of the world
The Sahara
Dusts out the grasslands.
The weary farmer

Starves in the ash of his crop.
Great bones
Of high-shouldered cattle whiten
Like standing stones.

And for us, wheat burns, crops
Are dug in,
Coffee beans thrown in the sea.
The financier's spin

Of the dice, the market, dictates.
Our charity, even,
Puts money in our purse.
Thatcher or Reagan

Give our kindness its voice.
But you, Brace,
Civil servant, bureaucrat,
The Janus face

Looking both ways to two worlds,
Serving the market
Yet knowing that in the wages you earn
Lurk plan and target —

In that mindful view of things that you
As bureaucrat
Know as the perfection proper to you,
Greed and waste like that

Should be impossible. Capitalists
May dump their goods,
Sink coffee or burn wheat; but good bureaucrats
Don't poison spuds.

A SQUARE OF GREY SLATE

presented to Pedro Pérez Sarduy, Cuban poet, at the Wales-
Cuba Resource Centre at the National Eisteddfod 1985, in
Rhyl.

Days I have been wondering, Señor,
How I should speak:
The very language I use being wrong
For Eisteddfod week,

And yet I'm not satisfied
To mumble it glumly
As a mere *lingua franca*
Between Cuba and Cymru.

My tongue's my own, True Thomas says.
How then
Can I speak in the crowding name of all Welsh
Women and men

To offer you, Señor, the brotherhood
Of Welsh Wales?
How can I strike red fire from the very iron
Of our chains?

This morning early, I went to my rainy garden
Hoping to find
A messenger — perhaps a riddle
Of times out of mind —

A palimpsest of my people, a forgotten tryst
That I could keep
For them this Monday morning
Of Eisteddfod week.

There in the path was this square of grey slate.
Let that stone
Be my herald, I said, let its mute cry down the years
Atone

For my English. Let it speak
Where I cannot
Of the Welshness of Wales
Now, on this spot.

Men die here for stone. The ancient strata eroded
By rain, by frost,
Till the massif's a mere negative
Of what it was . . .

Señor, stone is the stuff of oppression
In this land.
Look, the conqueror's castles, Rhuddlan, Rhuthun, Denbigh,
Still stand.

No one in Wales is untouched by rock.
Coal and slate
— Laid down before dinosaurs walked the world —
Dominate

Vast tracts of our industry, our past.
It was for stone
That the shanty-towns mushroomed
To chapel and home.

Rock was our vortex. Our working class
Was drilled from it.
Their dream and their discipline answered
The greed of the rich.

Strike. Lock-out. Depression.
Let this stone lip
Tell of those terrible years.
Now, slate-tip, coal-tip

Rear up like pyramids. Pharaoh and Israelite
Share
The memorial of the dump
Under wide air.

Welsh poets in love, Llywelyn Goch, Dafydd or Iolo,
Used to sing
Poems to thrush or tomtit, salmon or north wind
— Anything

Under the moon that moved, he'd make it
Ambassador,
Messenger, *llatai* for him, to travel
Straight to his girl's door

And tell her how much he loved her
And how much
He died, died for the sight of her,
Died for her touch.

Now therefore I command this square of grey slate
To go *llatai* for me
Through Westerlies and Trades
To the Carib Sea.

Go, little Fidelista of slate,
To the midmost
Of the Americas, where the plumes of royal palm
Mark Cuba's coast.

Go to the sugarcane fields, the rice paddies,
The orchards —
Go where the blacks once died like flies
As the cash flowed northwards.

And tell them, slateling, about our country,
This place of stone
At the edge of Capital's shadow
As the day comes on.

GOOSEBERRIES

For Mike Donahue, killed in a car crash August 1985

They sat in my bowl, globular, tawny
And so ripe
They wanted to burst. My fingers
Had burns in the grip.

When you pick them, prickles seem friendly
Like the kneading pins
Of a kitten in your lap. The bushes walk home to be milked.
Their udders swing

In the sun-tanned lanes. They demand that you
Pick them, pick them,
Every last berry that has bent
Shoot and stem

To the waiting earth. From the pricketty bush
All Saturday
My thumbs pulled gold. In punnets and bowls
Green gallons lay.

And that night I walked to the pub
Whimsical
From the gooseberries' rock 'n' roll
Festival.

"Mike, if you like gooseberries," I said,
"You can have a ton
For the taking." "Ah, they're lovely," you said, "grapes
With whiskers on!"

"They're over-ripe, bursting," I said, "but the flavour's
Too good to waste."
I watched your imagination bend to them
Savouring the taste.

"A bit of fermentation never did anyone
Much harm.
We'll come for them." A gooseberry tryst wafted
On the breath of barm

Bubbled quietly into your sleep. You had drunk
Well and happily
At someone's do. Promises could keep.
Time had the key . . .

But earth waits for fruit. That Sunday night,
Screams and tearing
Of brakes, hurtling of steel in the rain
And an end of caring.

I remember the hospitality of your presence,
How we came into it
As if we were lost in the cold, to a hearth where a wood fire
Has long been lit.

How you drew your world round you, layer on layer,
Round a fire
That you feared was anarchic at heart — could break out
Brutal and dire

With an open madness of suffering, to shame you
And leave you
Apprehensive of friends whose shocked kindness
Had tried to ease you.

Well, well. Gooseberries, like Irish harps,
Sing the sweeter
The closer they are to bursting.
World was completer

(So it seemed, Mike) for you then:
Marriage and job
And family, all rounded in some manner of peace.
The berries bobbed

On the leaning twigs, the songs were tawny with power,
The love could open.
I remember a friend, a singer, a lover of gooseberries
Gathered and broken.

Pardon me, therefore, if I keep this gooseberry tryst
Too late.
The fruit returns to the earth. Mike Donahue,
Peace be your fate.

A MILK TOAST

for Jean Gregson, newborn

Milks are distinguishable.
Our own wild kind
I've not tasted since times
Out of mind.

You've to work for it now,
Tugging to feed
At a gorged nipple
Playful with need.

For you — for most of us — soon
Milk will mean
Packaging, bottles or cartons
Sealed by machine —

Cow juice or dairy product,
Something to cloud
Black coffee or tea
To a palatable brown.

I am old enough
To have gone out
In a sweet-pea sort of morning
To a horse and cart,

A blue-striped jug in my hands
To be ladled full
From a churn with sliding whiteness
Not quite cool.

I pour a glass, remembering. Bubbles
Coagulate
For a second, then thin
Wretchedly and break.

But this, too, is milk — sterilized
Friesian stuff,
A lingua franca of dairies,
Minimal enough!

Oh, a lot talk of blood. Blue blood.
Sine qua non
Of lordly thugs. Hot blood
Of the torrid zone.

Flesh and blood. A matter of lacking
A proper cell wall
And therefore part of the minority kingdom,
An animal.

But we, from common crawlers, distinguish
Our mammary past.
In the night of the Saurian day, milk not blood
Gave us class.

Sucking is our definitive labour.
Lips and hands —
Both of them work to ensure that supply
Matches demand.

Suckle and suck: milk's reciprocity
Is primal.
Love shall always have lips for us now.
So long as we're mammal

Food shall be common ground,
Represent
For us potential of Agape,
Missa, what is sent.

The love-feast re-enacts lactation.
Communion
Or Christmas Dinner, both half-remember
That topless union.

Suckle and suck. Communicants
Of heart and lip —
Their proto-speech gathers as milk
Surges and dips.

(And indeed, our labial stops,
Fricatives,
Liquids and aspirate gasps
Are sucking's negative,

Pulled out instead of in, as speech
Gives new contexts
To the pillow-talk
Of mouth and breast.)

Birds warble with their throats. Crickets
Rasp wings.
A man learns the truth from our lips.
We are milk things,

And therefore, Jean,
For your birthday
I raise this glass to you.
May milk-light stay

For you always as sanity. May relationships
Be built
At lip-level. Be worthy, not of red blood,
But of milk.

A FERN FROM SKYE

for Somhairle MacGill-eain
        (Sorley Maclean)

'Lament for the children'
— a pibroch by Padraig Mór MacCruimein

I

We came across two worlds to see you, Sorley,
To Skye
The last battlefield, the last
Never say die

Of the Gael: the Celtic world squeezed out,
Cauterised for sheep;
Its leaders angled in sharp practice;
Highland and creek

Emptied of the tribes;
Croft and song
Left rotting like bladderwrack
On the high strand.

2

It was here, in Peinnachorrain of the Braes,
That the tenants held fast,
Met and showed fight. Broken head,
Clout and gasp

By their intransigence, refused
That grey day
At the sea coast, to be dumped
Or carted away.

Visitors we came. Clean air delighted us, gull music,
Cottages
Under the hill, clinking of little streams
And a damp breeze

From Raasay across the Sound. But you, you live here,
Poet, among
The presentative past of your people.
The old tongue

You teach to seed, in the imagination's
Freehold
To grow and in untoward time, to green bare rock
Like veins of gold.

3

To a tryst I'd come. For fifteen years
I'd fingered the coin
Of our one meeting together, kept our currency
Of talk warm

In the pockets of my heart.
Poet —
Greatest in these islands now — here's that groat for you,
Look, my hand holds it!

4

But your cottage was closed. You were away!
In the filtering light
Tangled woods and wet places
Of Raasay were bright . . .

But as I turned to join my children already
Racing down
In the joyous concentration of shingle and sand,
The shrill sound

Of them dimmed in the great space like oystercatchers',
Like peewits',
And their mother walking between them, drawing them
   after her
For all their tricks

Like a shepherd to the best pasture —
As I turned,
It was your wall caught my eye: the piled stones, stone-crop
And the mats of fern.

5

Male fern, was it? Branching stocks,
Stiff straight frond
Crinkled and each pinna upturned to the air — no,
It felt wrong! —

Dryopteris oreades then? Pioneer
Of high screes,
Not under a thousand feet, the books say,
Nor by the sea.

A highland plant, its distribution
Not fully known —
Not, certainly, expected in the sea-level
Stones of your home.

For a moment it seems like the Gael himself —
Its history
A lost unexpectedness, a perfecting
Entelechy

Informing the blue distances.
Not for it
The plush leafmould of a wood.
Rock its roots fit.

6

Rock. And a great music.
Apprehension
Of the fern resonating
To the taut scansion

Of that ground. Piper pulls the lament
Round him,
Walks the contemplative ways
The air has found him.

Slow measure of this music's
Magnanimity.
A reaching certainty. Sorrow
Between cloud and sea.

Each variation affects the light,
Each singling
Of gracenotes the geometry of this
Lament for the children.

For the children that are not.
For those died
In all ages, now. For those
In the hunger have died.

For the Gael who loses this music.
For the children.
For me, O Conaráin of the Curraigh,
This grace singling.

7

Oreades in the stone. Music's geometry
Along your wall
Makes interface. People with real names
Find your door.

The heart has freehold. Green veins
Of a poetry
Gold in the rock. Black roots
Between cloud and sea.

The children circle the beach. Their antennae
Gather
Treasure from the stones — a shell,
A curlew's feather . . .

I thought, you wouldn't mind. I widged
With my knife
A tiny crown — this fern — from the mat
Of its crinkled life.

It grows now by my kitchen window.
My daughters carp
As they come from school, their Welsh words
Tugged and sharp

And flown across its space like a kite
In the wind.
It uncurls in its own time still.
It chooses to sing.

BLODEUWEDD

A poem for dancing

for Michael Cullimore who painted her,
for Anna and Bronwyn who dance her,
for Ann Jenkins who listens.

I

I was begotten in the lure of bees.
Pollen sticks to my lips. I have the scent
That wings moths under the moon. Gametes of greenery
Double and clasp in the work of my eyes.

I am bastard of mead and moorland.
Wood-toughening shoots grew my memories tall.
Nakedness of flowers I had foisted on me.
In the puberty of stamens I learnt my way.

2

Was he my father? A point of light
Fabricates my being. A joiner —
A watchmaker, silversmith,
Locksmith, cheapjack conjuror. And here I am.

Was it like that? The beard of a man, the magic
Tune of a flute he held, a word he spoke —
I have forgotten. But by male insolence
I was usurped, a woman, a grown girl.

By a male charmer I was forged
Counterfeit woman. All the currency
Of the feminine he made lively
To pay for a home.

I was never by him given a childhood.
No one prospected my gibberish for words —
Mam mam, mam mam — or held their arms
For my first free steps. He never thought of it.

Nor by that magic of his was I ever joined
Egg and sperm, cell and cell
Within woman's nakedness,
Within the black woods, at the gates.

No tideflow of bodies suddenly stilled,
No stifled cry
Began me in hiatus beyond yearning,
Cell for cell, across the wetlands.

No harrier, quartering the fen, hunted.
No elvers filed through the alluvium

Of smooth streams, from the wild Sargasso
To home in on me with their gift of death.

Singularities were not led to that church,
Cathedral'd Ely in the wine-dark marsh.
He took the sex of meadowsweet and oaks,
The flaming orgasm of broom, to conjure.

3

The glances of my husband Lleu follow me round.
His eyes soften when I look at him. I like that.
I look at him quite often. Sometimes it annoys me.
Sometimes I stare at him. I sulk in my stare.
He is half conscious of it. His eyes look hurt.

My husband Lleu is a great man around town.
He has top people for friends. Apparently
They like me. Their eyes soften when I look at them.
Rather, perhaps, they like the fact of me.
The think me suitable for Lleu.
My beauty decorates their admiration for him.

I walk in the streets of the town.
I do not know what to say to the townspeople.
So far, because I am young, they do not mind.
Their eyes follow me with approval.
I take care to smile at them shyly.

My husband Lleu comes into our bedroom.
His hands reach out. They dandle my hair.
He kisses my cheek, my throat, my lips.
His fingers wedge my frock over my shoulders.
They slip it along my arm. My breasts show.
As he touches them, as he kisses them, my breasts
Start up like hares. Sit high and watch warily.

My frock clutters my feet. I step out of it.
My husband Lleu makes me lie down. His hands
Dance on my buttocks, round my thighs
And all up my spine. I like it when they dance.
My husband Lleu puts his lips in odd crevices.

His kisses snatch and suck, snatch and suck.
I feel his swollen tube warm against my crotch.
I touch it with my long fingers. We move together.
My husband jerks inside me, moves, moves, moves.

I cannot separate what happens.
I am giving a token of having been loved.
My husband Lleu and I sleep in the one bed.
His friends approve of it. I am suitable for Lleu.

4

Oakleaves are glazed with summer.
Translucent red infancies are
Fired to thick shards of green.

A stag lurches out from the trees.
Eyes at the last reach of terror
Brush past me without acknowledgement.

My thighs stiffen, my head rotates.
I look for the hunter, smile
To his insolent salute. He will kill,

That much is certain. And this too —
I shall take steps to meet him.
I have a sudden hunger for meat.

5

Faggots burn under cauldron.
Hounds curl before hearth.
A mouse glints in the corner.

My breasts stretch up like birds.
My eyes half open, my jurisdiction
Is a coquetry decorative as leaf.

His footfall comes through the wood of me.
He opens the tarred door
Into the chipped gloom, like sunlight.

We play like weasels. Sudden as kitten,
Pat-a-cake, twirl, claws out,
Still as a sleeping trice,

Nowhere away. Peregrine stalks
In our play, preens a long plume,
Gentle my tiercel, swift as dream.

Bear cubs walk, roll
Like sailors to fisticuffs,
Tumble an armful, pretend to gnaw.

We wheel like buzzards together.
We mew in the Spring wind.
I am fledgling of blood.

6

The death of a hero like Lleu comes in kit form.
You have to assemble it, learn the jargon,
Familiarise yourself with all the bits.
Finally, you find the directions do work.
There's a funeral to prove it.

Such a death, like a crossword, finishes
Without sense of climax — the last clue no less glib
And flattering to the solver of it
Than every other. And yet, this one and not that
Fetches the death. The knife disembowels him,
The bullet reaches his heart, he commonly dies.

Death might lie fallow for years, all but one item
Complete in it. Patiently, like stamps,
It has to be collected. It acquires value
From demand, from the rarity of a full set.

Such a man's death is compiled like a dossier.
It sets a precedent. As my lover
Writes the last entry in, hurls the barb
That a year of Sundays fashioned
In the time the priest said mass, at a man
Who is neither indoors nor out, neither
On horseback nor on foot, but poised
In the absurdity of allowing it to happen —

As my lover hurls the spear, he knows
That by the common law of heroes
This precedent shall kill him also:
Neither indoors nor out, neither
On horseback nor on foot, with a spear

That a year of Sundays fashioned
While Father Dwyer was saying mass . . .

He had known it, really, the first time
He noticed me. It was part of the finesse
And the humour of our courtship.
He now hurls the spear, knowing
That no boulder will protect *his* groin,
No limed figure-of-eight shield, tightened
From the whole hide of a bull, will ever guard *his* heart.

7

I was standing near my husband Lleu
When the spear struck him.
I was paying attention. I was interested
When the spear caught him.
I was asking him for precision
When the long spear struck him.
He was demonstrating for me. He was laughing
When the enormous spear gutted him.

I was so near I saw the sky explode out of his eyes.
I felt the jerk of his buttocks like an earthquake.
I heard the blood of his belly scream on the ground.
I smelt the urine of fright cloud the bright air.
I was so near I tasted his salt.

And in those infinite moments before my lover
Raced down the riverbank, scattering goats,
Hardly daring to exult, not believing in it,
Yet running towards the two of us, the dead Lleu
And me his wife crouching by the side of him —

In those vast moments I saw — or perhaps I saw
For my sights were out of joint, the infinite world
So flared in my turning eyes — perhaps I saw
Wide fingering wings and bare claws below them,
A grey head, a slow sweeping beat
Of a wounded eagle making for trees.

And I heard — didn't I say I heard? — the high squeal
Of the bird like lightning in the echo of Lleu's scream,
Scream within scream, for as long as those moments.

My lover came to me. I stood to meet him.

8

Detectives are sniffing the long grass,
Treading down meadowsweet, measuring
The girth of alders and the rooting capacity
Of sallows and osiers. How tipsy was this fern?
Can that horsetail be trusted to give evidence?
Who killed Cock Robin?

Gwydion the Chief Inspector's not satisfied.
Though he was the boy's father, he's wangled it
To be put on the case. The powers-that-be
Are trying to hush it up, my lover has friends
And his administration is popular. No one else
In the circumstances wanted it.
The way was open for Gwydion, giver of fantasies,
Reader of dreams.

He rides at the head of a host, the grey man,
Fast as thought through every fastness,
Climbs slow as sleep the terrible gorges,
Dives through the wounded rivers of Britain.

His is the superintendance of corpses,
The interrogation of dust. On his shoulders
Two young ravens cough their secrets.
They fly out, counting dead flesh.
The grey cloak twitches as they home to him.
Gwydion, Old Hoodie, blind in one eye,
Croaks to his chicks for carrion they find.

The old man looks everywhere for his son.
Now he is riding, witchdoctor and warlock
Of the tribe of Venedoti, through the woods

And slate-tips of Nantlle by Segontium.
His knees press the plump stomach
Of a nice-natured mountain pony plodding through
    ramsons
Like a tinker. On the pony's backside
Twelve shrunk heads of warriors jangle.

Gwydion rides naked to war, dust on his skin
Decorated by wounds and blue woad
In the necessary uniform of police inspectors . . .

And meanwhile I grow round with my lover's baby.

9

I am in fruit, and ripen with the year.
There is a cave of whispers in me.
Old women look wise about it.

I go between absurdity and wonder,
Between nausea and content.
My skin is no longer a solitude.

On precarious thin legs
And trotting like an unsheared ewe
I busy myself with daydream and sleep.

Sudden activity floods me like wishes.
My surfaces, all but one, soften
And I taste different to myself.

Is it finally womanhood
That this burrowing magician under my breasts
Buds into me at last? Is that my peace?

10

Gwydion is cultivating a hobby,
An inordinate passion for hogs.
Pig-craft is all he can talk about —
Elmet White Swine, Old Spots of Gloucester,
Tamworth boars and Cornish Large Blacks.
He hangs in speculation over a sty,
Endlessly debates of brawns and lards,
Runts, yilts, yolks, yangled shots . . .
They say Gwydion is "settling down" —
The constabulary are embarrassed by it.

I tell you, a sorcerer is like a child:
Quiet, or elaborately obvious,
And you expect trouble. Precisely then
It is perilous. Gwydion watches pigs —
How they wait for the swineherd to free them,
Trample and squawl into the woods, and root
Happily all day for acorns, truffles, corms,
Tubers, tumbled birds, blind mice and snails,
Whatever the Lord of Pigs made edible.
One sow alone is beyond computation.

Gwydion is learning that Sow, like a language.

I I

Where was the Sow born?
> Under the hill. Under the hill.

How many in the litter?
> Twelve and twelve. Twelve and twelve.

Who owned her sty?
> Sun and moon. Sun and moon.

Where did she wander?
> Through the wilderness of the world.

How fast did she run?
> Quick as fear. Quick as greed.

Where did she hurry?
> To the World's End, in Nantlle.

What did she end with?
> A tree. A tree.

What did she guzzle?
> Gobs of flesh. Maggoty flesh.

12

And Gwydion put on the speed of his fantasy;
He buttoned about him fictions of light.

His mastery of dream was on his feet;
He conjured distance by sleight of hand.

His eye took on the pig. He heard her squealing
Like the path of a shooting star in heaven.

Twice he attempted it. Twice her gallop
Outran fancy, beggared his thought.

A third time, though, he was at the sty
When the swineherd unlatched her. His eye was ready.

The third time the teller of tales ran clear
With the gross Sow of time, fleet as she.

And he stood at last under the close web of twigs
Of the tree that the Sow haunted, and smelt

The rotten flesh as it dribbled down to earth
And heard in the dead calm an eagle sigh.

13

Gwydion concentrated his stare into the branches.
Like a cat hunting he settled himself.
His hand from time to time touched absent-mindedly
Shoot and leaf in the undergrowth. His tongue
Flickered between his teeth; now and then
He mewed softly with excitement.
Never did he relax the narrowness of his eyes.

Suddenly he was singing: a long howl of words,
Unbelievably loud falsetto
With the urgency of a god in it:
Screaming like an eagle, yet precise and deft,
Eagle to eagle, till nothing in the whole valley
Had any authority except this scream.

The cry turned living and dead to artefact.
Nakedness served for a conduit
And the long gusher pushed between lean ribs, into air
Shocked and washed clear by the sound.

He sang to the oak. In the intensity of it
His hands grew leaf, fingers plumped from bud.

The Sow had learnt her manage; and my body,
Twenty-five miles away, was shaken and bruised.

14

The police say that the Chief Inspector
Recovered my husband's body actually alive.
They say despite severe wounds, malnutrition,
Shock and great weakness, Lleu lives.
A communiqué says he is in intensive care.
He has taken some gruel. The doctors
Are optimistic. But what is worrying
Is that his mind
Appears deranged. He talks of eagles.
He is convinced that the Chief Inspector
Is some variety of falconer.

He stoops to the lure.

15

Rowan heath, bilberry scrub.
Wildcat on outcrop of rock
Searching, cantering like a wolf.

Red kite dips, swerves on a bend
And up. Turn and hurry of murderers.
Scree and low cliff. Wild cat and red kite.

And towards me the Sow lurched
Headlong through the birch thicket,
Her clutching nose singling me out.

Her snout nuzzled me. Suddenly
The terrible teeth closed on my crotch
And I fainted in my drowning child.

16

And for months after I would dream the birth —
I who had never borne baby, dreamt it
To the last detail. Head locked, waters
Broke, the first dull twinges shuddered
Into the long crescendo of openings —
Every convulsion of it, and the ticking pause
Between each pain. At every turn
The mind's worry reverberated
In the womb's voiding of itself
Until anxiety and pain were paradigms
Each of the other. I dreamt it over and over,
Always the same, until within the red mist
Crowning the well of birth like an oracle
The head showed. All paused for that sacred thing
That stood miraculous, unbodied
Between the uplifted, mountainous thighs.
The stalkless head must turn to left or right
Before the birth easily, easily
Proceeds . . .

                    But in my dreams that moment
Ended in contraries. Sometimes I'd wake then,
Only be certain of the head's birth, not the rest;
Sometimes the head would have no body to it,
Roll over like an egg, lose nose and eyes,
And wait for my warmth to hatch it.
I could sense the night in it, the chick
Growing towards a darkness that no vegetation
Can tolerate long or feed from. My memories
Being oak, are of bright air and water,
Being meadowsweet and broom, are sunshine and high
     cloud.

I sense my exile from the light of day
By the dark fumbling within that egg.

In other dreams, the head, as it was born,
Would partly split, and from its top
A root would twist, query my stomach
For entry, nuzzle down. From the emptying cranium
Two seed-leaves pulled, strap-like,
Into second birth. Before my eyes
I'd watch a sapling sprout. Bird or oak,
My dreams depleted me of womanhood. I'd wake,
Sweaty and shamed, avoid even my love's eye.

17

Through the little summer of michaelmas
Birches with drunken pointillism
Leaf by leaf, silver and gold, turn yellow.
Bracken sings red to the matt green of gorse.

The oaks are corked down for the winter.
Orgies of acorns in their cups
Gravel the ground, the dry leaves
Beginning to stagger.

We have put pickets out on Gwydion
To watch where he goes. It is hard, though,
To resist the drunkenness of the trees
In this fool's paradise of michaelmas.

My lover denies anything is wrong.
He is moody for days. Why won't he tell me
He has a walking, breathing dead man on his mind?
A hunter's superstition gnaws the bad luck of it.

He leaves me more and more to my hysteria,
Makes circuit of his lands, dealing
Rough justice to badger and fox,
And drinking late in tavern and stews.

Rumours are mad like wasps. One day
We will all fly out, and die
On the warm stones: before the sun
Is too weak to thaw our brittle wings.

18

The young girls run in panic.
They've heard Gwydion is coming.

He has the story-teller's fancy for us.
Subtle his charm, sharp his knife,

Master of halt and leap
In the craft of coincidence,

Shaman of shifting form,
Huntsman of nuance and trickery —

He has his eye on us. He'd cut a girl's throat,
Toss her aside as easy as a rabbit.

We run to the mountainside, looking back.
Climb the sharp scree, hide in rocks.

Young girls in dirty tatters,
Cold and tired, stripped by bramble,

Watched by the bone cups of lichen,
By the golden knobs of the moss.

I have killed his son. Grief
Is the name and bent of the fable.

I have killed Lleu his son. The title
And aim of his tale is death.

19

Suddenly the cloud strikes. Nowhere
Is every path, rock and rock. We're lost
In a freezing whiteness, our thin frocks
Clammy with drizzle. Reverberations
Deafen us. We huddle together.

Rock and rock. Ledge. Cliff. Debris
Of rock. Every noise is Gwydion.
The cloud mows us down like chainshot.
We run from a tinkling goat, looking back.
Below us, arms outstretched, the waiting lake.

20

Till the thaw, till the calm dawn, my body
Lay in the water a thousand years.
Finally the lake rejects me. Unseasonable
Petals lie like ghosts on the wet stones.

In that underwater meadow of quillworts
Oak I was made of pleaded with dank grit
To send down roots for me, throw off the graft
Of humanity, let it properly wither
Like the incubus it was, and strike,
Grow trunk and leaves, and in this desolate place
Be tree again, feed on the bright air.
Meadowsweet too, and casual wood of the broom
Stirred in that dream of water, were layered
In sifting mud, and poked warm rootlets out
Into the shock of thaw. Before I rot
Let me establish here, and taste the light . . .

No, the lake has spurned me. I am too glib with flowers
To grow in its deep refuge. Quillworts
Are in the outermost orbits of chlorophyll
Before the dark. "Meadow" we fancifully call it,
Seeing their tufts like grass or daffodils;
But to themselves, they are "the People", aboriginal
Trees of the earth, the first Rain Forest,
Sigillaria, Lepidodendrons
Of the Coal Measures. They have lost all stem,
All but the fruiting cones and the roots —
Their one trust being the lineage.
This lake is an imperium
Shrunk to a backyard. But in it
My rooting is too brash. Oak-writ does not obtain.

On the down-wind shore-line of the lake
Broken quillwort leaves lap the gravel.
Even whole corms have been torn by the icy
Fathom-rake of the wind from the mud bottom
To lie now, whitely green, in a devastation
Naked to the air. And with them, the dead
Bodies of girls float or strew the shore.
Enid, her frock bunched up to her shoulders,
Shows a cleft rump to the morning. Eigr,
Once with green eyes, is attended to
By an assiduous crow. Elen and Luned
Grind pretty noses to the merciless stone.

But my body the lake rejects. I sit upright,
Already an old woman, my skin
Puffy and flecked with seepage. My two eyes
Are wild with the death of those round me.
My hair is white. All my colour's leached out.
My legs are thick with fluid, every joint of me
Aches with the poisonous cold. No one
Would want me. My sex is a lost dryness
Beyond the stars. I gingerly try to stand.

There, in the gateway of the morning, Gwydion comes.

21

Suddenly the lakeside was like a fairground
Flooded with people. Stretcher-parties
Put down their poles in the geometric
Order of those about to build booths.

Tents were pitched, tea brewed, piles of blankets
Laid in cubes. Each drowned girl
Was inspected, hoisted with tackle.
Doctors gave them rough lessons
In how to breathe — only they didn't.
Detectives searched for evidence of intent.

I think the god, Old Hoodie, spoke with me.
Horns of a bull slanted out from his brows.
Two indifferent ravens on his shoulders
Listened as he banished me from light.

Was it like that? The beard of a man,
His eye holding my eye, a word he spoke —
I have forgotten. But it is male judgement
Turns me away. Darkness usurps me.

Afterwards, though, I notice
No one is cross. Policewomen
Help me to walk. Their eyes look embarassed,
Tender perhaps. Nurses fuss round me,
Inject my legs. I am made ready
To be moved into permanent dark.

For already under my skin I could feel
The bones re-grouping, hollowing out.
Along their delicate corridors
Air moved easily. And on my skull

Ear-sockets shifted, one up, one down,
The better to take bearings, asymmetrical.
Enormous eyes looked out from mine.
I was lithe, predatory, soft.

Now, blinking with stage-fright, patiently
I sit, a pathetic, dumpy heap
Of dowdy feathers, twitching with fear.

But under the dishevelled down on my legs
The steel claws accurately turn.

I wait without scruple or remorse.

BLODEUWEDD

Programme note for the New Zealand production, 1983

Once upon a time, a woman was created out of flowers. She was not born in the way we are born, but made by the art of a sorcerer, a magician. She was a woman, yet not a woman; she had no mother to find her womanhood in. This is her story. In the poetry that follows, she will speak.

The legend says that she lived in the mountains of North Wales, on the wet and windswept Western seaboard of Britain. The rock of these mountains is very old, contorted and buckled, glaciated and worn down. At present the land is mostly bare of tree cover, but then it was probably oak scrub or birch forest, except for the tops of the mountains. There are many lakes, high tarns and rivers. Water has dominated and shaped this land for as long as it has existed.

The legends of the country are like the rock: ancient, eroded, very often confused. The tale of the woman made from flowers — Blodeuwedd — was apparently written down in the twelfth century; but nobody knows how old it was then. Her husband, Lleu Llaw Gyffes, or Lleu of the nimble hand, was probably a pre-Christian Celtic god. Her story may be pre-Roman; or it may be simply a mediaeval folk-tale that has been glued into the fabric of myth. But in either case, it is old enough. These are not modern fancies but legends of men and women long past.

Blodeuwedd's story is part of a collection usually called *The Four Branches of the Mabinogion*. Actually it is from the Fourth Branch, the tale of Math vab Mathonwy, and a most extraordinary tale it is, woven of magicians and sexual lust, a king being betrayed and a queen's curse circumvented. Magical shape-shifting is almost a way of life in this story. Within about twenty pages we hear of stallions and greyhounds being made for one day out of toadstools; of men being made into deer and wild swine and wolves —

66

and both male and female ones at that; of a girl made out of flowers; of her husband being killed and flying away as an eagle and then spelled back into a living man once more; and of the flower-woman, Blodeuwedd, finally being changed into an owl. What immediately catches our eye in this strange tale is the superfluity of changes, the sense of the solidity of human personality all the time dissolving into animal forms.

If we found this sense in the psychologist's clinic, we would call it schizophrenic. And partly our apprehension of Blodeuwedd in the poetry that follows is that she is mad: she lacks an emotional structure to make her human, she fails to achieve true womanhood. In one sense this is a poem about a girl going insane, becoming an owl, a thing of darkness.

But in another sense, of course, it is a poem about a legendary story. For reasons that are too complicated and confused to go into now, Lleu Llaw Gyffes, Lleu of the nimble hand, has been cursed by his mother Arianrhod that he will never have a wife of the race of women that is now upon the earth. To avoid this curse, Gwydion his father (or some say his uncle) who is a magician makes for him a beautiful girl, Blodeuwedd, out of the flowers of the oak, meadowsweet and broom. Lleu marries this woman, and for a time they live happily together. One day, though, when Lleu is away from home, a stag stumbles past Blodeuwedd, closely pursued by Gronw Bebyr the hunter. Blodeuwedd and Gronw fall in love and plot to kill Lleu. She finds out from her husband the only way in which he may be killed: that is, with a spear that has been a year in the making, fashioned only during the times that the priest is saying Sunday Mass. He can be killed with this spear if he is neither indoors nor out, and neither on horseback nor on foot.

Lleu explains to her that the conditions would be met if an open-air bath-tub had a thatch put over it and a billy-goat was fetched to stand alongside it; and if he, Lleu, were to stand with one foot on the edge of the bath-tub and the other on the billy-goat's back. If someone had the right kind of spear when Lleu was doing this, Lleu could then be killed. "Why," says Blodeuwedd, "I thank God for it. That may be avoided easily." But she tells Gronw her lover, and he goes off to make the spear.

A year later, Gronw comes back with the spear and lies in wait. Blodeuwedd says to Lleu that she is still worried about the manner of his death: she does not understand how the conditions may be met. Lleu laughingly agrees to a demonstration — to act out, in fact, his own fashion of dying. As he balances on the bath-tub and the billy-goat's back, Gronw hurls the spear and Lleu is killed.

Lleu is killed; but something of him is left, which flies away in the shape of a wounded eagle. His father, Gwydion, goes in search of him. Gwydion is a magician, a witchdoctor, a craftsman. He is also (in the story) a poet and a storyteller, a creator of fiction, one whose weapon is pre-eminently the imagination. He has created Blodeuwedd out of flowers; now, like a police detective, he has to find out who has killed his son.

Gwydion stays one night with a swineherd and notices that one of the sows rushes out every morning and no one can follow where she goes. Gwydion is intrigued and attempts to follow the sow, which, with his magic strength, he manages to do. He finds that she rushes off to an oaktree growing between two lakes, and that she is feeding from decaying flesh and maggots that continually fall out of the leaves of the tree. Gwydion looks up to the tree and guesses that it is Lleu whose wounded body is dribbling down to the sow. Gwydion sings to Lleu in the tree, and the wounded eagle hops down, first one branch then another, finally into Gwydion's lap. Gwydion strikes the eagle with his magic wand and it turns into the thinnest and most dilapidated man you ever saw. It is Lleu, and Gwydion takes him home and for a whole year cherishes him until he is strong again.

At the end of a year Gwydion and Lleu set out to punish Blodeuwedd and Gronw Bebyr. Gronw is away from home at the time, and Blodeuwedd flees into the mountains with her maidens. They are so busy looking behind them, frightened to death by the thought of Gwydion coming after them, that they fall into a lake and all but Blodeuwedd are drowned.

Gwydion the magician catches up with Blodeuwedd and says to her: "I will not kill you. I will do to you what is worse. I will let you go in the shape of a bird. And because of the dishonour you have done to Lleu Llaw Gyffes, you shall never dare to show your face in the light of day. And there shall be enmity between you and all the other birds, so that they will mob and molest you wherever they find you." So Blodeuwedd becomes an owl; and that is the reason why all owls have faces like flowers.

Meanwhile Lleu and Gronw, Blodeuwedd's husband and her lover, confront each other. Gronw agrees that Lleu should aim his spear at him, in the identical spot that Gronw had aimed his at Lleu; but as he was led astray by a woman, he begs Lleu to let him interpose a boulder of rock between them. Lleu agrees to this, but it does Gronw no good at all. The spear goes right through the rock and Gronw is killed.

Approximate Pronunciation of the Names

Blodeuwedd — Blod-dáy-weth (*ay* as in *day*, *th* as in *with* not as in *kith*.

Lleu Llaw Gyffes — Llay Llow Gúff-ess (*ay* as in *day*, *ow* as in *cow*; there is no English equivalent to the Welsh *ll*, though the *tl* in *antler* is something like it in rapid pronunciation. Put the mouth in the position for saying *l* and then hiss. It differs from *l* as *s* differs from *z*.

Gwydion — Gwid-yon

Gronw Bebyr — Grón-oo Béb-ir

Nantlle (originally Nantlleu, Lleu's brook) — Nánt-llay (*llay* as *Lleu* above).

Enid — Én-is (En as in *pen*)

Eigr — rhyming with *vaguer*, with a trilled *r*.

Elen — Él-en (*en* as in *pen*)

Luned — Línn-ed (*ed* as in *Edwin*). The Welsh form of Lynette.